An opini

RAINY DAY LONDON

Written by
EMMY WATTS

INFORMATION IS DEAD.
LONG LIVE OPINION.

When we conceived these guidebooks, we feared they would fail. Who needs a guidebook when everything can be googled for free?

But then it occurred to us; that's exactly why you *do* want a guidebook. You want lively, trustworthy opinion combined with great photographs. You don't want endless information from a thousand online bots.

We think you are like us: you care about quality, you care about style, you care about provenance, but you don't have time to waste on long words like 'provenance'. You want to cut to the chase: where's good?

If you were to come and stay on our couch (it's a metaphor btw; we have a guide to hotels), these are the places we'd recommend – even if it's p*ssing down.

Ann & Martin, co-founders
Hoxton Mini Press

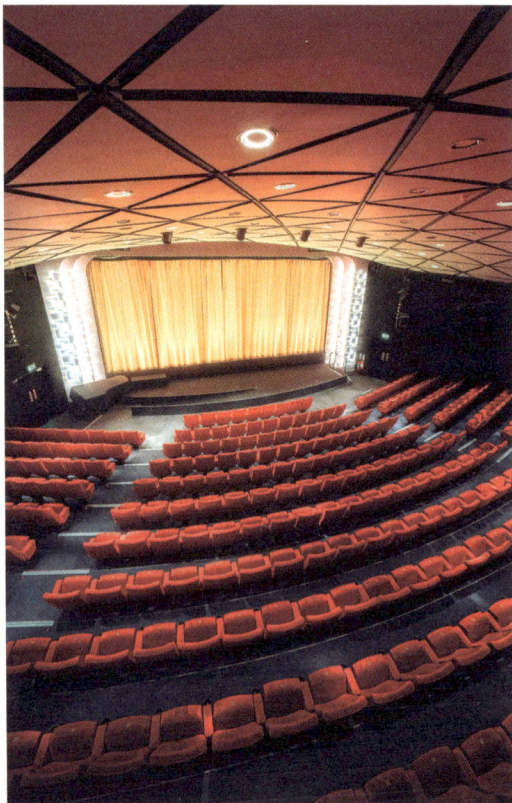

BFI Southbank (no.32)
Opposite: The Barbican (no.4)

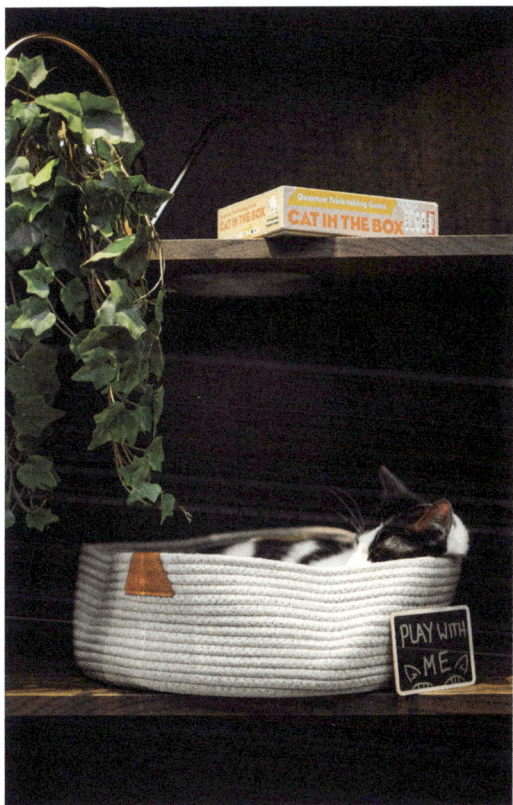

Java Whiskers (no.38)
Opposite: V&A East Storehouse (no.17)

Swingers (no.48)
Opposite: Social Pottery (no.55)

THE GREAT INDOORS

London is a rainy city. At least, that's what we Londoners would have you believe. Ever eager to wax lyrical on the weather, we've forged a reputation as a city of brolly-toting, welly-wearing, cagoule-stashing deluge dodgers – never happier than when we're having a good moan about the rain ruining our plans/mood/blowdry.

So intense is our passion (or disdain) for precipitation, we've built an entire vernacular around it. (As London's unofficial mascot, Paddington Bear, put it, 'Londoners have 107 different ways to say "it's raining".') But while it might seem like it's perpetually coming down in stair rods – or whatever your chosen idiom – London probably isn't half as wet as you might imagine. In fact, both Rome and Paris experience more rainfall each year, and you don't hear anyone calling either of them rainy cities.

Still, with an annual average of 164 days of rain in the capital, it pays to be prepared for a downpour. Thankfully, London's got you covered – quite literally. As well as 1,000+ permanent exhibition spaces, 3,500+ pubs and numerous covered shopping outlets, our fair city counts a 95-year-old indoor ice rink (no.37), the UK's only indoor rollercoaster (no.50) and an indoor rainforest (no.4) among its airtight amusements, so you never need to worry about a shower spoiling your fun.

Speaking of which, we've got more weatherproof gaming spots than you can shake a joystick (or old-school die) at.

Whether you want beer and board games (no.21, no.54), or coffee and consoles (no.43), rain never stops play at these happy-go-lucky haunts. And don't worry if thrashing your mates at *Scrabble* or completing *Super Mario Bros. 3* isn't your idea of a good time. We've got cafes dedicated to virtually every niche, from the art of collage (no.26) to unadulterated feline adoration (no.38) – ideal for when it's raining cats and dogs.

Don't get us wrong, London is heavenly in the sunshine. As a city made up of nearly 50 per cent green space, we give great 'great outdoors'. It's just, we think we do indoors even better. And while it might not be the rainiest city, it's by far the best city in which to spend a rainy day, whether you're sitting out the storm in one of its many cosy boozers, swerving a shower at one of its world-class galleries or even watching the drama unfold from its loftiest public viewpoint (no.9).

London might have a reputation for its rain, but never in a million years could it ever be accused of being dry. So don't wait for the storm to pass. Grab your brolly and get out there. Or, y'know, *in* there.

Emmy Watts
London, 2025

Emmy Watts is a London-based writer and blogger who's authored a dozen books for this series. She's spent the best part of a decade finding ways to occupy her two daughters on rainy days, though the sound and smell of a downpour are two of her favourite things.

BEST FOR...

Soaking up some culture

London's cultural scene is endlessly inspiring – even when the weather isn't. Visit Tate Modern (no.22) for contemporary art in a dramatic setting, V&A East Storehouse (no.17) for a new way to experience art and design or Japan House (no.47) for a taste of Tokyo.

Training in the rain

You don't need the great outdoors to get a great workout in the capital. Get your endorphins flowing at one of Roller Nation's (no.49) rollicking roller discos, on Yonder's (no.20) epic bouldering wall or on Queens' (no.37) all-weather ice rink.

Kids climbing the walls

No sun needn't mean no family fun. Zoom down Britannia Leisure Centre's (no.51) spiralling flume, pay a visit to the Science Museum's (no.33) Power Up gaming lounge or ride on London's only indoor rollercoaster at Babylon Park (no.50).

A sans-brolly browse

Fancy a spot of retail therapy without the damp dash between shops? Make a beeline for the capital's dazzling department stores and covered markets, be it Liberty (no.46) for fashion and floral fabrics, Alfies Antique Market (no.57) for heirloom treasures or Rough Trade East (no.15) for music and merch.

Rainy-day refreshments

Nothing cheers a gloomy London day like a cosy pub – and with its hearty British fare, The Pelican (no.39) is one of the best. Craving more international flavours? Visit Seven Dials Market (no.3) or Mercato Metropolitano Mayfair (no.41) for everything from bao buns to burritos.

Embracing the deluge

Only happy when it rains? Take advantage of a squally situation, whether you're swimming in the rain at central London's only heated open-air swimming pool (no.5) or enjoying a bird's-eye view of a particularly dramatic downpour from the giddy heights of Horizon 22's (no.9) 58th-floor viewing deck.

Cloudbusting escapism

Alternatively, transport yourself somewhere else entirely, be it the world of your favourite director at the capital's best-loved indie cinema (no.7), inside the mind of satirical cartoonist Tim Hunkin at his madcap gaming arcade (no.6) or to actual heaven courtesy of London's oldest day spa (no.45).

Staying all day

When it's really bucketing down, you need all-day entertainment under a single (watertight) roof. BrewDog's (no.23) vast flagship boasts a slide, bowling alley and on-site ice-cream van. The Barbican (no.4), meanwhile, packs art, performance spaces and a lush tropical oasis into its concrete shell.

1

HIDDEN LONDON TOURS

Secrets of the Underground

Clouds equal crowds as far as the London Underground is concerned, but don't hail that cab just yet. Instead, book yourself onto one of London Transport Museum's behind-the-scenes Tube tours and dodge the downpour and the droves – all while gaining a fascinating insight into the capital's secret history. Choose from 12 different 90-minute tours shedding light (both literal and figurative) on everything from long-disused 'ghost' stations and those reputedly haunted by actual ghosts, to deep-level wartime shelters and bomb-proof bunkers. As an added bonus, you can use your tour ticket to bag 50 per cent off entry to the museum – another wet-weather haven boasting three fun-packed floors of vintage vehicles and hands-on displays.

Various locations
ltmuseum.co.uk/hidden-london

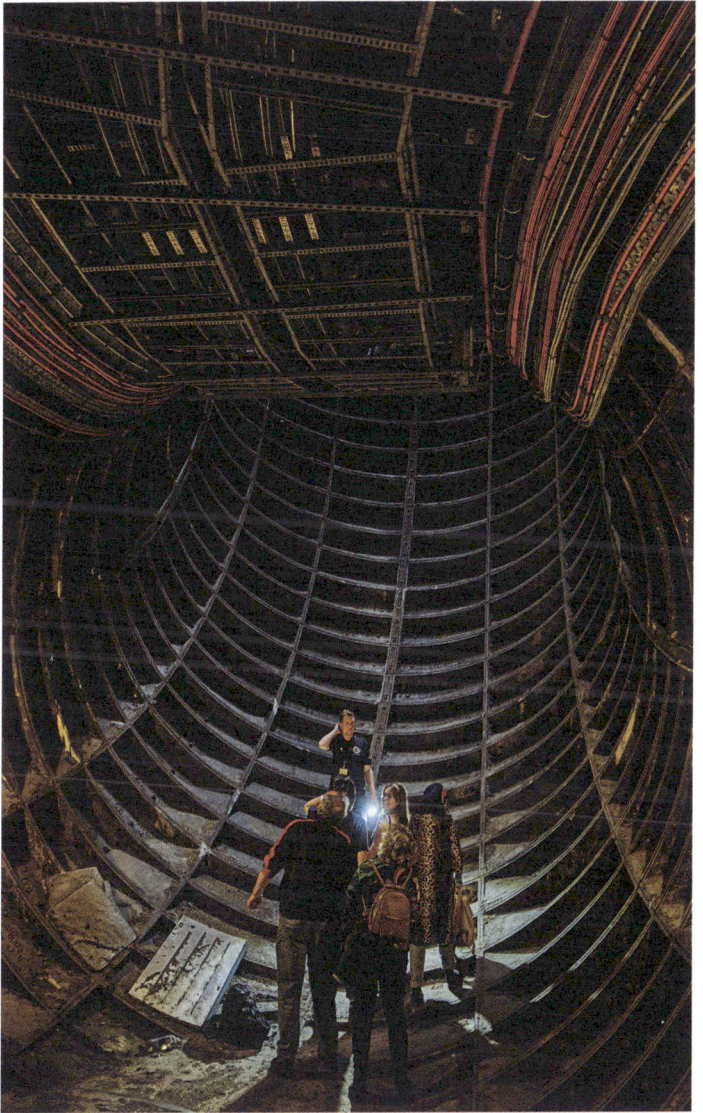

2

THE NICKEL

Grindhouse microcinema

You *could* spend a rainy day mindlessly mainlining new releases at your local cinema chain. Or you could spend it devouring cult treasures you won't find anywhere else at this gutsy grindhouse gem. Specialising in bizarre, banned and low-budget films, this 37-seat newcomer is partly funded by film-lovers, who in turn are free to devise their own outlandish programmes – be it a John Waters season or a body horror fest. Fancy some dystopian anime deep-cuts, a Soviet psycho-horror or some zero-budget Eurotrash? Then you may have discovered your niche. Rock up early for pints, vinyl listening and a rummage through the rare-movie merch store in the vibrant basement space.

117–119 Clerkenwell Road, EC1R 5BY
Nearest station: Chancery Lane
thenickel.co.uk

3

SEVEN DIALS MARKET

Hip food hall serving diverse street eats

There are food halls – and then there's Seven Dials Market. More akin to an upscale culinary department store than your average dining court, this hungry person's haven could comfortably sustain a full day's guzzling, with its 20 indie restaurants and food stalls, duo of vibey bars and plethora of places to park your bum (without it getting soggy). Choose from kati kebabs from Kolkati, stupidly spicy sandos from Lucky's Hot Chicken, frozen karma coladas from Bar Nana and piccalilli-topped Caerphilly from the world's first cheese conveyor belt (or save yourself the agony and order something from every stall). Look out for seasonal offers and occasional live acts lighting up the bubblegum-pink stage.

Earlham Street, WC2H 9LX
Nearest station: Covent Garden
sevendialsmarket.com

4

THE BARBICAN

Sprawling Brutalist arts centre

Where better to ride out a rainstorm than in London's best-loved Brutalist fortress, the 40-acre, free-to-enter Barbican Centre? Within its reassuringly chunky concrete walls, brolly-bypassers can traverse a tropical oasis that's home to more than 1,500 species of plant (check the site for Conservatory open days); browse a vast library of books, scores and songbooks; and soak up a vibrant programme of film, music, theatre and art in its cavernous cultural complex. The site's generous smattering of bars and cafes ensures you can stay all day without so much as getting drizzled on, but if you're willing to run the risk of sideways rain, proceed to the covered portion of the highwalks for some elevated architectural observation.

Silk Street, EC2Y 8DS
Nearest station: Barbican
barbican.org.uk

5

OASIS SPORTS CENTRE

Exhilarating outdoor pool

Head to Holborn's only open-air pool in a heat-wave and you'll be treading water with everyone who lives or works in a two-mile radius. Amble down on a drizzly day, however, and the 80-year-old lido really lives up to its name. Open and heated to a comfortable 25.5 degrees Celsius whatever the weather, this central London sanctuary is surprisingly serene in a downpour, when all but the most hardcore bathers steer clear. You'll be left blissfully alone with nothing but your thoughts, the elements and the soothing patter of raindrops for company. The adjacent covered pool offers a welcome backup for squallier days, while the poolside sauna is the ideal spot for a post-dip defrost.

32 Endell Street, WC2H 9AG
Nearest station: Tottenham Court Road
better.org.uk

6

NOVELTY AUTOMATION

Absurdist amusement arcade

No matter how dismal the weather, this delightfully daft attraction is sure to cast some satirical sunshine on your day. The life's work of engineer, cartoonist and all-round legend Tim Hunkin, the kooky Holborn hangout invites you to embark on the world's shortest minibreak from the comfort of a motorised armchair, receive telephonic relationship advice from velvet-voiced crooner Barry White – and even secure a quickie divorce. You'll need to purchase around £30 of tokens to experience each of these weird and wonderful machines, but if you're button-bashing on a budget, then the ever-surprising Expressive Photobooth, slobbering Test Your Nerve dog and surreal Chiropodist encounter should all be non-negotiable.

1a Princeton Street, WC1R 4AY
Nearest station: Holborn
novelty-automation.com

CHIROPODIST

INSTRUCTIONS

1 REMOVE SHOE, BUT NOT
   SOCK, FROM FOOT TO BE
   TREATED

2 POSITION FOOT IN
   TREATMENT BAY

3 INSERT COIN IN SLOT

TIM HUNKIN 84

7

PRINCE CHARLES CINEMA

Movie-lover's mecca

Its unofficial slogan might be 'sod the sunshine, come sit in the dark', but this beloved 1960s movie theatre is delightful whatever the weather. The only independent cinema in Leicester Square (albeit lurking down an alley in characteristically noncon-formist style), the two-screen venue is prized for its diverse programme, showcasing everything from blockbusters to B movies and cult classics to new releases. It's also famed for its reasonable prices and a sense of filmic fanaticism that sees it host quote-alongs, sing-alongs and even all-nighters on the regular. Sign up for lifetime membership as a matter of urgency, and keep an eye on the website for mystery movies, director seasons and plenty more to keep you on the edge of your seat.

7 Leicester Place, WC2H 7BY
Nearest station: Leicester Square
princecharlescinema.com

8

RENA SPA

Recharge your batteries

Burrowed in the basement of an airy four-star hotel, this zen boutique spa is the ultimate cure-all for a miserable day. Quietly luxurious, with its 25-metre pool, infinity-edge jacuzzi and tranquil sauna and steam room, the subterranean sanctuary will make you forget the time of day – let alone the weather. Despite its plushness, Rena regularly ranks as one of London's best-value spas, meaning you can double up on treatments, be it an aromatherapy massage and an anti-ageing facial or a nourishing body wrap and luxury pedicure. Or, if all that chilling leaves you peckish, treat yourself to a post-pamper afternoon tea (with bubbles) in the laidback hotel bar.

Leonardo Royal Hotel London City,
8–14 Cooper's Row, EC3N 2BQ
Nearest station: Tower Hill
Other locations: multiple, see website
renaspa.co.uk

9

HORIZON 22

Skyscraping viewing gallery

Granted, London looks lush on a sunny day. But nothing beats the dramatic beauty of the capital in a thunderstorm – particularly when witnessed from its loftiest public viewpoint. Perched on the 58th floor of the UK's second-tallest building, this two-storey observatory promises jaw-dropping vistas from its 300-degree windows, with views stretching far beyond the City, even in cloudy conditions. Hop into the high-speed lift for a heart-stopping thrill ride from 0 to 833 feet in just 41 sensational seconds, then sit back and admire the view – coffee (or champagne) from the resident cafe in hand. Browse the events schedule for pop-up yoga classes and sound baths, or just check the weather forecast for guaranteed theatrics.

22 Bishopsgate, EC2N 4BQ
Nearest stations: Bank, Liverpool Street
horizon22.co.uk

10

THE NATIONAL GALLERY

Marvel at European masterpieces

While the hordes flock to its hallowed halls on inclement days, the recent refurbishment of the National Gallery's spacious Sainsbury Wing – not to mention the masterful rehang – has made visiting this renowned art institution a much more satisfying affair, come rain or shine. Leave a drizzly Trafalgar Square behind and proceed to the 18th-century galleries in search of some much more picturesque wet scenes: those of Canaletto's Venice. Or make your way to the Modernist zone to gaze upon van Gogh's turbulent, swirling skies – counterbalancing them with a generous slab of cake from the homely on-site restaurant. Bringing the family? Don't miss the state-of-the-art Roden Centre – a wet-weather haven for crafty kids.

Trafalgar Square, WC2N 5DN
Nearest station: Charing Cross
nationalgallery.org.uk

11

FAIRGAME

Grown-up funfair

Fancy all the fun of the fair, minus the kids, naff prizes and unpredictable weather? Roll up, roll up for London's adults-only indoor fairground, a 20,000-square-foot funhouse where revellers aged 18+ can battle it out across nine tech'ed-up twists on carnival classics. Try your hand at whack-a-mole with gophers, a grown-up donkey derby and a coconut shy you wouldn't take your nan to, and be rewarded with something slightly more sophisticated than a goldfish in a bag (think prosecco-infused candyfloss or even a ski trip, if you're lucky). When your winning streak's over, tuck into tantalising tacos, towering burgers and generously topped pizzas, all helped down with a cheekily named cocktail. 'Small Duck Energy', anyone?

25–35 Fisherman's Walk, E14 4DH
Nearest stations: Canary Wharf, West India Quay
Other location: St Paul's
wearefairgame.com

ALLEY HOOP
BUMPER BAR
SPRITZES
HARD LIQUOR
PANTRY PANDEMONIUM

12

BAR KICK

Shoreditch sports pub

Want Premier League and pints? F1 and fried chicken? Cricket and cocktails? Whatever your game, get your kicks at this vibrant neighbourhood bar – a two-storey sports fan's oasis inside a converted Victorian ironworks. Part of the local landscape for nearly 25 years (an aeon by Shoreditch standards), this ever-popular spot is home to not one, but *twelve* giant 4K screens showing up to three games at any one time, as well as foosball tables and interactive dart boards in case you want in on the action. Fuel up for a day of fixtures with a wrong-but-so-right peanut-butter-loaded Fat Elvis Fun in a Bun (burger) and delectably dirty Truffle Shuffle Cheese Fries. Book ahead, or you'll kick yourself.

127 Shoreditch High Street, E1 6JF
Nearest station: Shoreditch High Street
urbanpubsandbars.com/venues/bar-kick

13

K1 SPEED KARTING

Rip-roaring go-kart racing

While we obviously wouldn't recommend any form of outdoor racing in wet weather, this indoor go-karting hub promises stimulation, speed and safety for ages 8 and above, whatever the forecast. Operating state-of-the-art, all-electric go-karts across a sinuous 800m track, this former underground carpark is by far one of the most thrilling spots to pass a damp day in the capital, with top kart speeds approaching an exhilarating 45mph and plenty of hair-raising bends to navigate. When the chequered flag comes down, pull into the trackside restaurant for sustenance worthy of an F1 pro, from tender wings to loaded nachos – plus plenty of prosecco for the victor.

15 Cabot Square, E14 4QS
Nearest stations: Canary Wharf, West India Quay
k1speed.com

14

ALL STAR LANES

Old-school bowling alley and diner

Escape rain *and* reality at this Brick Lane bowling alley, whose retro games, vintage vibes and decadent diner grub will instantly catapult you back to 1950s USA. Whether you're down for karaoke and classic cocktails, towering burgers and ten-pin bowling, shuffleboard and sharers or pizza and *Pac-Man*, this vibrant venue is your rootin' tootin' one-stop shop. Perfect for parties, All Star Lanes is known for its all-star offers, from seasonal sales and happy hours to discounts for families, students and large groups, so you can afford to stay long after the skies have cleared. It's the American (drizzly day) dream.

95 Brick Lane, E1 6QL
Nearest station: Shoreditch High Street
Other locations: multiple, see website
allstarlanes.co.uk

15

ROUGH TRADE EAST

Legendary music store and venue

More than just a record store, Rough Trade's Tardis-like flagship is London's alternative-music mecca. A Shoreditch institution since 2007, the 5,000-square-foot space offers plenty besides idle vinyl flipping, with its on-site cafe–bar, sizeable book and biography section and compact stage, hosting a packed live-performance programme (recent crowd-pleasers have included beabadoobee, Little Simz and Soccer Mommy). Supposing you *are* just here for the vinyl, you're still in for a real treat, courtesy of a vast, genre-spanning selection featuring everything from funk to folk and country to krautrock. Don't head out into the downpour without checking out the merch (the own-brand caps are cool *and* rain-friendly) and bagging yourself a Rough Trade-stamped photo-booth strip as a souvenir.

Old Truman Brewery, 91 Brick Lane, E1 6QL
Nearest station: Shoreditch High Street
Other locations: Soho, Notting Hill
roughtrade.com

16

OLD SPITALFIELDS MARKET

Vibrant food and shopping mecca

There's something for every mood and palate at this legendary covered bazaar, which has been trading as a market since Charles I granted a licence for 'flesh, fowl and roots' to be sold on the site in 1638. While you'll still find all three available, courtesy of the 40+ restaurants and stalls that peddle everything from burritos to bubble tea, this is more than just an amazing lunch spot. Be sure to browse its cornucopia of independent boutiques and select chain stores hawking quirky clothing and homeware, plus its seriously rummageable antiques, fortnightly vinyl market and packed programme of events. There's no need to bring a brolly, but you'll almost definitely require a tote (or two) for your acquired treasures.

16 Horner Square, E1 6EW
Nearest station: Shoreditch High Street
oldspitalfieldsmarket.com

17

V&A EAST
STOREHOUSE

Art-and-design giant's trailblazing archive

There are hundreds of London museums in which to while away a wet day, but this humongous Stratford newcomer is poles apart from the rest. Resembling a vast IKEA warehouse, this cultural vault turns the museum-going experience on its head, granting visitors an edifying peek behind the scenes of the V&A's extensive archive, as well as the chance to order an object for a one-on-one appointment with any item of their choice. Across four inspirational floors, contemplate the world's largest Picasso, a slice of a now-demolished Brutalist housing estate and a spectacular 15th-century carved ceiling from Torrijos Palace. Don't miss the museum's new David Bowie Centre, which houses the musician's out-of-this-world archive.

Queen Elizabeth Olympic Park, Parkes Street, E20 3AX
Nearest station: Hackney Wick
vam.ac.uk/east

18

MUSEUM OF
THE HOME

Hands-on history of the home

It's fitting that the world's first museum dedicated to life at home should feel so... homely. Free, interactive and unfailingly welcoming, the former Geffrye Museum (renamed to cut ties with the infamous slave trader) is the kind of place you could hole up in all winter and never get restless. While the gardens are glorious on balmy days, the interior is inviting all year round. Head to the hands-on Home Galleries for Victorian housemaid role-play or Super Nintendo on the sofa, or poke around their 12 immersive 'Rooms Through Time' – recreations spanning a 17th-century parlour to a 1970s British-Caribbean family living room, and even a flat from the future. Kids in tow? Don't miss the family reading lounge and cosy sensory den, then exit via the design-led gift shop.

136 Kingsland Road, E2 8EA
Nearest station: Hoxton
museumofthehome.org.uk

19

BRICK LANE
VINTAGE MARKET

Vast underground fashion bazaar

Want to shop one-of-a-kind fits, support independent retail and save the planet – all without risking mane frizz? Step forward this vintage-vulture's paradise, which peddles everything from Y2K handkerchief tops to 19th-century corsets, via vinyl go-go boots and polyester shell suits – all under one concrete roof. This eclectic emporium is the largest of its kind in Europe, with around 100 stalls operating out of the vast basement space, seven days a week. Seek out Urban Trenches for upcycled Burberry coats, Lovalo for one-off designer finds from the '90s and Noughties and Circus Vintage for Victorian capes, blouses and puffy 1980s ballgowns. Or simply spend an entire, gloriously damp day rummaging through the lot.

85 Brick Lane, E1 6QL
Nearest station: Shoreditch High Street
vintage-market.co.uk

20

YONDER

Climbing and coworking space that rocks

Wide blue yonder looking decidedly grey? This vast and visually stunning bouldering hub promises a grand adventure to rival the great outdoors – minus the unpredictable weather. Arranged across a spectacular three-tiered amphitheatre, this hip hangout triples as a yoga studio and flexible co-working space, complete with an on-site cafe and bakery run by local dough demons Wild Grains, so you can carb-load all day without ever encountering the elements. Day passes and pass packs make visiting cost-effective and flexible for newbies, while a jungle-themed mini climbing room and giant top-out slide will delight mini mountaineers and big kids alike.

4–6 Hooker's Road, E17 6DP
Nearest station: Blackhorse Road
thisisyonder.com

21

DRAUGHTS

Buzzy board game cafe

Ready to up your (board) game? This playful cafe–bar's elevated comfort eats, encyclopaedic drinks menu and impossibly well-stocked games library are guaranteed to brighten your day. Located in the vibrant Leake Street Arches complex – London's longest legal graffiti space – Draughts welcomes players of all ages and abilities, whether you're popping in for a round of *Battleships* and bao buns with the kids, or settling in for an afternoon of cocktails and *Cards Against Humanity* with your mates. Don't know your *Catan* from your *Carcassonne*? Draughts' dedicated gaming gurus will gladly recommend the perfect game for your party – and even offer some handy hints along the way.

Arch 16, Leake Street, SE1 7NN
Nearest station: Waterloo
Other location: Stratford
draughtslondon.com

22

TATE MODERN

Contemporary art colossus

London's cathedral of culture pulls in the crowds whatever the weather, with plenty to sustain an entire day (and sometimes night) of art appreciation. Beyond the free collections – whose displays offer an accessible introduction to modern art from 1900 to the present – Tate stages around six major ticketed exhibitions annually, showcasing the work of everyone from Andy Warhol to Zanele Muholi, across diverse movements and media. A veritable playground for cooped-up kids, the gallery hosts a family-friendly digital-drawing studio alongside imaginative children's art workshops, while its 35,000-square-foot Turbine Hall invites endless frolicking. Grown-ups, meanwhile, mustn't miss its monthly Tate Lates – after-hours art nights with DJs, performances and workshops under one roof.

Bankside, SE1 9TG
Nearest stations: Blackfriars, Southwark
tate.org.uk

23
BREWDOG WATERLOO

Mammoth beer hall with family amusements

Scottish pub chain BrewDog operates approximately 75 venues across the UK, but when it comes to whiling away a particularly grizzly day, there's only one you need on your radar. Nestled beneath Waterloo station, this 27,500-square-foot funscape draws families and big kids in their droves, with its storey-spanning tunnel slide and six-lane duckpin bowling alley. First and foremost a beer hall (complete with an on-site microbrewery), this bumper branch boasts a whopping 60 taps, plus a mega menu of burgers, wings and pizzas (and cleverly dubbed kids' 'Hoppy Meals') to soak it all up. Finish with a Hackney Gelato doughnut sando from the resident retro ice-cream van… but maybe give it a minute before getting back on that slide.

Unit G, Waterloo Station, 01 The Sidings, SE1 7BH
Nearest station: Waterloo
drink.brewdog.com/uk/brewdog-waterloo

BREW
WE ARE CARBON NEGATIVE.
LAGER & PILSNER
CIDER
ALCOHOL FREE

24
BOROUGH MARKET

Vast culinary offering under one roof

Many a London Bridge-bound Londoner has ducked beneath Borough Market's barrel-vaulted roof to dodge a downpour, but this 4.5-acre epicurean utopia is a rainy-day destination in its own right. Poised to keep you sated, quenched and entertained for hours, this historic foodie haven is home to more than 100 stalls and restaurants dishing up delicacies across countless cuisines – and they're not stingy on free samples. Proceed to Palma for silky salume and buttery burrata, jaunt to Jamaica for condiments with a kick, then bus over to Buenos Aires in pursuit of dulce de leche-stuffed alfajores (sweet, gooey cookie sandwiches) – all without so much as dampening your fringe or clocking up any air miles.

8 Southwark Street, SE1 9AL
Nearest station: London Bridge
boroughmarket.org.uk

25

BATTERSEA POWER STATION

Fun, food and shopping in an electrifying space

At its peak, this iconic brick behemoth generated 20 per cent of London's power. Now in its easy-going era, the former workhorse has been reincarnated as south London's premier retail, leisure and culture destination, offering top-notch shopping, dining and entertainment. Inside the Grade II*-listed building, browse boutiques such as Reformation, Space NK and Aesop, before pulling up a barstool and sinking an energy-themed cocktail in one of the landmark's former control rooms. Next, embark on a thrilling elevator ride to the top of one of those famous chimneys, followed by posh kebabs from Le Bab or tender noodles from BAO. Brought your brolly? Discover DNA VR arcade, visit The Cinema in The Arches and enjoy copious other experiences just a short, soggy sprint away.

Circus Road West, SW11 8DD
Nearest station: Battersea Power Station
batterseapowerstation.co.uk

26

PAPER STORIES

Quirky crafting cafe

With its fire-orange frontage, colourful collaging kits and friendly vibes, this creative community cafe is the joyful antithesis of a wet and windy day. Always buzzing, despite its relatively quiet location, this erstwhile post office welcomes drop-in crafting for all ages, as well as offering grown-up workshops by night (with wine, if that helps get your creative juices flowing), private paper-craft parties or just an inspiring spot to relax, fuelled by doorstep sourdough sarnies. The hand-risographed collaging kits make great greetings cards, for a gorgeously personal result every time. Crafting skills not up to scratch? Fear not – they also have a beautifully curated selection of ready-made cards to buy.

234a Gipsy Road, SE27 9RB
Nearest station: Gipsy Hill
paper-stories.co.uk

27

SOUTHBANK CENTRE

Landmark riverside arts complex

While its leafy rooftop bar, skittish play fountain, mouthwatering food market and legendary Skate Space have confirmed this lively arts centre's reputation as a solid sunny-day hangout, its iconic concrete roof facilitates plenty of foul-weather fun. Dodge the deluge with some cutting-edge contemporary art from the inimitable Hayward Gallery, a cathartic concert in the capacious Queen Elizabeth Hall or some thought-provoking theatre at the labyrinthine Royal Festival Hall. Should you be swerving a more sudden shower, the centre's copious cafes, design-led gift shops, comprehensive poetry library and busy programme of diverse drop-in events should keep you entertained while the storm passes.

Belvedere Road, SE1 8XX
Nearest station: Waterloo
southbankcentre.co.uk

28
CHISLEHURST CAVES

Atmospheric tours of an underground city

Weather so dismal you want to crawl into a hole? This subterranean labyrinth will keep you warm, dry and engaged for the best part of an hour, courtesy of a captivating lamplit tour of its meandering, 22-mile tunnels. Used for mining since the Neolithic period, these hand-excavated caves are thought to date back more than 8,000 years – though arguably it's their recent history that's most engrossing. The tiny church and hospital built to cater for the 15,000 souls that sought shelter during The Blitz are still in situ, brought back to life by a band of merry mannequins, and there's still evidence of the stage where rock legends Pink Floyd, The Rolling Stones and David Bowie once raved in the caves.

Caveside Close, Old Hill, BR7 5NL
Nearest station: Chislehurst
chislehurst-caves.co.uk

29

BRIXTON VILLAGE

Vibrant market with international flavour

The beating heart of Brixton for nearly a century, this covered market – formerly known as Granville Arcade and Market Row – has seen its fair share of rainy days, surviving everything from WWII bombs to the Brixton riots to the abiding threat of demolition. Still, the Grade II-listed arcade remains one of the most exciting places to chow down in the capital, boasting a veritable smorgasbord of cuisines: think Jamaican seafood, Japanese pancakes, vegan Thai street food and Venezuelan arepas, all under one big steel truss roof. When you're suitably sated, walk it off with a browse of the bounteous indie stalls selling everything from vintage clothing and homeware to diverse books, plus plenty of traditional traders hawking fresh produce from far-flung climes.

Coldharbour Lane, SW9 8PS
Nearest station: Brixton
brixtonvillage.com

30

PECKHAM LEVELS

Hip hangout in former car park

An old multistorey car park may not sound like the most inspiring place to pass a drizzly day, but ascend Peckham Levels' famous kaleidoscopic staircase and you're in for a cloudbusting treat. Home to more than 80 independent businesses dishing out everything from Senegalese soul food to psychotherapy and locally brewed beer to lash extensions, as well as housing private studios, this ten-storey concrete colossus throbs with creative community spirit from its ground-floor music event space to its (admittedly less weatherproof) summer rooftop bar. Damp days call for foosball in the food hall – complete with views over south London's stormy skyline – or, for those with tots in tow, for *really* good coffee in the highlighter-hued play area.

95a Rye Lane, SE15 4ST
Nearest station: Peckham Rye
peckhamlevels.org

31

FOUR QUARTERS

Consoles, cocktails and comfort food

Whether you're partial to *Pac-Man*, have a soft spot for *Street Fighter* or delight in *Donkey Kong*, this easygoing arcade bar is everything your retro gaming dreams are made of. Home to more than 20 lovingly restored original arcade and pinball machines, two big-screen gaming setups and four indoor console booths, all playable using the venue's eponymous (and purchasable) US currency, this spacious hangout is bursting with nostalgic charm. When the rain sets in, settle down with your console of choice and a burly, bacon-crowned Bowser Burger or chilli-topped Sonic the Hedge-Dog, washed down with a mellow pint of Four Quarters Pale or a regal Princess Peach rum cocktail. A guaranteed win, whatever the score (or weather).

20 Ash Avenue, SE17 1GQ
Nearest station: Elephant & Castle
Other locations: multiple, see website
fourquarters.bar

32

BFI SOUTHBANK

Haven for film buffs

You can't beat a movie marathon on a less-than-clement day, but this film fan's fantasyland is a far cry from your average cinema. Occupying a glass-clad edifice on the South Bank that connects to the cylindrical IMAX building via a subterranean tunnel, the complex contains enough movie magic to fill several lifetimes of rainy days. Get your filmic fix in the suitably cinematic Reuben library – home to the UK's largest collection of moving-image-related books; inside Mediatheque's free-to-access booths and archive of over 180,000 films; or via Britain's largest cinema screen. Time to hit pause? Take a browse around the centre's well-edited gift shop or stop for a drink in its dramatic balcony bar.

Belvedere Road, SE1 8XT
Nearest station: Waterloo
bfi.org.uk

33

SCIENCE MUSEUM

Hands-on history of innovation

With its copious interactives, quartet of cafes, exhibits embracing the entire universe (and beyond) and an almost complete lack of windows, this mammoth museum was basically built for rainy days. Across its seven fun- and fact-filled floors, curious explorers of all ages can escape to other worlds via the IMAX cinema, game the day away in the Power Up arcade, lose themselves in the newly-launched Space exhibit and then find themselves again in the Who Am I? gallery. Kids can enjoy hours of indoor play in the hands-on Wonderlab and bafflingly named basement 'Garden' – though beware, the latter's giant water table is just as likely to drench them as the downpour you're escaping, so be sure to bring spare clothes.

Exhibition Road, SW7 2DD
Nearest station: South Kensington
sciencemuseum.org.uk

Birth of the
modern airliner
↑

Transforming
the Wellcome Wing

34

DESIGN MUSEUM

Inspiring exhibitions in spectacular space

At the very least, you'd hope that this Kensington museum's hyperbolic paraboloid roof would keep its visitors dry, but there are countless more reasons to pass beneath its soaring copper curves. While its flawlessly curated blockbuster exhibitions examine everything from Tim Burton to Barbie and skateboards to saris through a design lens, its Matthew Williamson-designed restaurant is an all-day brunch destination by itself, plating up seasonal sustenance in a luminous space overlooking Holland Park's 54 acres. Its gift shop, meanwhile, is one of the capital's best, often spilling out into the adjoining pop-up space to coincide with the museum's primary exhibition, while its extensive and enlightening free displays will keep you engaged long after the storm cloud has passed.

224–238 Kensington High Street, W8 6AG
Nearest station: High Street Kensington
designmuseum.org

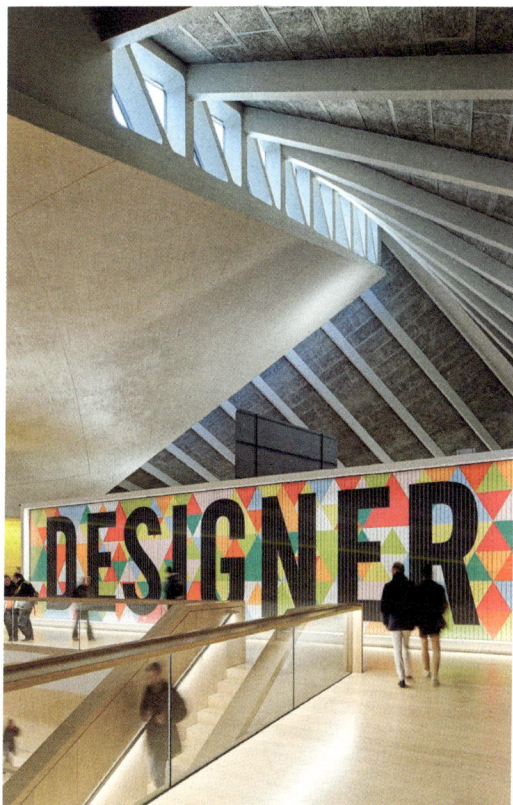

35

VICTORIA & ALBERT MUSEUM

Maze-like museum of creativity

One of London's most magnificent spots to get lost, the labyrinthine Victoria & Albert Museum is perfect wet-weekend fodder. A virtually endless source of inspiration, its colossal collection spans nearly five millennia of human creativity across everything from fashion and photography to sculpture and silverware, while sell-out exhibitions have delved into the enchanting worlds of David Bowie, Christian Dior and Alice in Wonderland. The breathtaking Cast Courts – home to a replica of Michelangelo's *David*; the Great Bed of Ware, known for its bawdy history; and *Tippoo's Tiger*, a curious 18th-century musical automaton, are all great places to start – but not before you've fuelled up with an indulgent cream tea from the gilded (and world's first) museum cafe.

Cromwell Road, SW7 2RL
Nearest station: South Kensington
vam.ac.uk

36

DAUNT BOOKS

Iconic bookstore with travel focus

As per its name, this Edwardian bookshop can feel intimidating, with its vaulted ceiling, oak galleries and insistence on arranging its titles by country, regardless of genre. But brave a browse and you'll find yourself caressing the covers of tomes you'd never otherwise have found, whether you pop in for a potted guide to Cape Town and leave with the complete works of J.M. Coetzee, or swing by for a Paris guidebook and depart with an unputdownable biography of Victor Hugo. Indeed, while Daunt is renowned for its travel literature, you don't need to be plotting a round-the-world excursion to peruse its shelves – visit for everything from classics to cookbooks and plenty more fodder for future rainy days.

83–84 Marylebone High Street, W1U 4QW
Nearest station: Baker Street
Other locations: multiple, see website
dauntbooks.co.uk

37

QUEENS

Subterranean playground with a historic ice rink

While the bulk of London's ice rinks only pop up for the festive season – and then close again the moment the weather takes a turn – Bayswater's 95-year-old indoor rink (London's oldest) welcomes skaters all year round, come hail or heatwave. Queens' spacious, icy idyll is a day out in its own right, but there's plenty more to this underground amusement hub, from interactive darts to on-ice curling, a retro gaming den and 17 bowling lanes for all-day sporting fun. When you're all played out, on-site diner MEATliquor's towering burgers, liberally loaded fries and scrumptiously saucy wings will have you feasting like those eponymous queens.

17 Queensway, W2 4QP
Nearest station: Queensway
queens.london

38

JAVA WHISKERS

Cat cafe on a mission

The ultimate antidote to a cold, wet day? How about an army of warm, soft cats poised to be played with, petted and generally adored? *Purr*-fectly luxurious, with plush soft furnishings and wall art depicting famous faces with their felines, this cosy cat cafe doubles as an upscale rehoming centre (each of its fluffy inhabitants is available for adoption). Prefer high-energy cat hangs? Book the kitten lounge. Or kick back with some of the cafe's more senior residents in the relaxed cat lounge. Select a 55-minute time slot or a longer, more relaxed experience (depending on the weather and your ability to tear yourself away) or go all out with an epic afternoon tea. Just remember, no sharing with your furry friends.

105 Great Portland Street, W1W 6QF
Nearest stations: Great Portland Street, Oxford Circus
Other location: White City
javawhiskers.co.uk

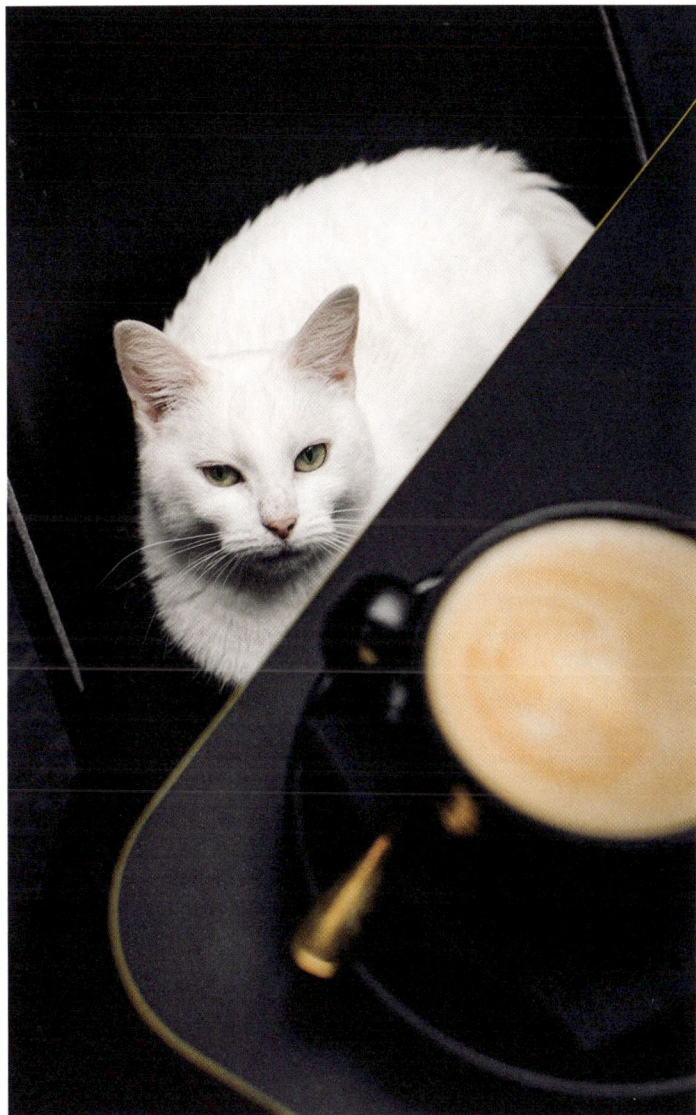

39

THE PELICAN

Posh pub, hearty grub

It's pubs like The Pelican that make you yearn for rain. Low-lit and laid back, with a roaring fire in winter and satisfying small plates year-round, this Notting Hill bolthole is the stuff of wet-weather dreams, serving up cosy country-pub vibes within spitting distance of Portobello Road. Take a seat on one of the buttery leather banquettes and order as many bar snacks as you can stomach, from oozy Welsh rarebit to sweet and meaty spider-crab toast. Or, if the rain's set in for the day, take advantage with something substantial – think showstopping tomahawk steak or lamb shoulder to share, eased down with something bold and fruity from the encyclopaedic wine list. Either way, fill your beak.

45 All Saints Road, W11 1HE
Nearest station: Westbourne Park
thepelicanw11.com

40

THE WALLACE COLLECTION

Maximalist Marylebone mansion

It's home to works by Velázquez and Canaletto, one of the world's finest hoards of arms and armour and a collection of furniture that once belonged to Marie Antoinette, and yet this central London townhouse is a lesser-known gem of the city's museum scene. Still, a nose around the sumptuous former home of the Marquesses of Hertford makes for a superb wet-weather diversion – its jewel-toned wallpaper alone promising to cheer up even the greyest of days. Arrive early to give its vast array of riches the attention it deserves, making time for a mooch around the current temporary exhibition before devouring a cream tea to the sound of raindrops beneath the courtyard cafe's colossal glass roof.

Hertford House, Manchester Square, W1U 3BN
Nearest station: Bond Street
wallacecollection.org

41

MERCATO METROPOLITANO MAYFAIR

Heavenly fare in deconsecrated church

A sense of spirituality is not a prerequisite for seeking refuge in this former church, but spend a soggy Saturday sampling its ambrosial offerings and you'll leave well and truly enlightened. In keeping with its opulent, Grade I-listed surrounds and ritzy neighbourhood, this temple of tasty treats is a cut above your classic food hall, with stalls specialising in everything from lobster rolls and freshly shucked oysters to award-winning sushi and matcha margaritas. Give the roof terrace a swerve in favour of small plates in the equally picturesque nave, followed by a lazy browse in the Nunhead Gardener's verdant foyer concession, or a cloudbusting glass of wine in the cosy crypt.

St Mark's Church, North Audley Street, W1K 6ZA
Nearest station: Marble Arch
Other locations: Wood Wharf, Elephant & Castle
mercatometropolitano.com

42

BRICKLAYERS ARMS

Historic pub with cosy corners

There are few things as dismal as Oxford Street in the rain, but make a damp dash to this back-street boozer and all is instantly forgiven. Dating back to Georgian times (not Tudor, as the timber framing might have you believe), the appropriately brick-clad Sam Smith's pub offers a welcome pit-stop for soggy shoppers and wet-through office workers, beloved for its sofa-filled upstairs lounge where the fire is seldom unlit. Granted, it's neither a destination pub (space is snug) nor a pub-roast venue (it's closed on Sundays), but the Brickies' cheap pints, classic comfort grub, back-room darts and friendly resident Cocker Spaniel make this classic alehouse one of the finest places to pass a wet day.

31 Gresse Street, W1T 1QS
Nearest station: Tottenham Court Road

43

CHIEF COFFEE

Games cafe in a Victorian bottling factory

Saving the good people of Chiswick from bad-weather-induced boredom for more than a decade, this friendly mews cafe offers rainy-day fun over three airy floors. On the ground, settle down on an Isokon Plus chair – a nod to the days when the iconic furniture company called the building home – and dig into a cream-dunked cinnamon roll or seasonal bake, washed down with speciality coffee from a tasty lineup of top-tier roasters. Next, head to the basement pinball lounge – host to an ever-changing roster of eight colourful machines themed around everything from *Stranger Things* to *Street Fighter*. Or, if Japanese arcade rhythm is more your thing, advance to the attic for a serious *Scotto* or *Maimai* sesh.

Turnham Green Terrace, W4 1QU
Nearest station: Turnham Green
chief-coffee.com

44

JAPAN CENTRE

Authentic East Asian food court

When the weather leaves you yearning for more exotic lands, board the bullet train (or the Northern line) to Leicester Square for a taste of the Land of the Rising Sun. Here, Japanophiles can fill up on fluffy hirata buns and crisp pumpkin croquettes in the meticulously presented *depachika* (basement food hall); pig out on pillowy mochi doughnuts from the dedicated cafe; slurp shochu sour cocktails and bold broths in the retro ramen restaurant; or sample world-class sake at the sommelier-staffed bar. Spend all day (and probably all your money), but don't leave without loading up on everything from panko breadcrumbs to Pocky sticks and manga magazines in the well-stocked shop.

35b Panton Street, SW1Y 4EA
Nearest station: Leicester Square
Other locations: Shepherd's Bush, Stratford
japancentre.com

45

THE PORCHESTER SPA

Traditional Turkish bath experience

Sombre skies got you craving some TLC? Look no further than this 1920s bathhouse, whose blissful treatments, balmy air and exquisitely preserved Art Deco interiors will promptly transport you to sunnier climes. A fiercely kept local secret despite its splendour, London's oldest spa offers top-to-toe pampering on a shoestring, with passes granting a full day's access to the traditional Turkish bath facilities at a fraction of typical prices. Take it easy in the (warm) tepidarium, find calm in the (warmer) caldarium, loaf in the (hot) laconium and sweat it out in the steam rooms and sauna before cooling down in the plunge pool, then starting all over again. Need a little extra attention? Book a deluxe massage or facial for added indulgence.

Queensway, W2 5HS
Nearest station: Royal Oak
everyonespa.com

46

LIBERTY

Idiosyncratic luxury lifestyle emporium

Nothing cheers up a dreary day like a bit of retail therapy, and this centenarian department store is easily London's loveliest. Purpose-built from the timbers of two decommissioned ships, the distinctive mock-Tudor mecca offers a one-of-a-kind shopping experience, laid out to resemble an (albeit palatial) home, complete with individual rooms, wooden panelling and fireplaces for a cosy, stay-all-day vibe. Across five enticing (and wonderfully creaky) floors, browse luxury beauty, gourmet gifts, designer clothing spanning Ganni to Gucci and impeccably curated homeware – not forgetting those iconic Liberty fabrics. Fuel up between levels with seasonal small plates at plush eatery Seventy Five, and mark your diaries for the annual unveiling of the much-loved Christmas shop – the origin of many an heirloom bauble.

Regent Street, W1B 5AH
Nearest station: Oxford Circus
libertylondon.com

47

JAPAN HOUSE

Upmarket cultural hub

Jonesing for a Japanese adventure? Why wait for sakura season (or splurge on extortionate air fares) when you can get your fix slap bang on Kensington High Street? Arranged over three immaculate floors, this stylish cultural centre is your one-stop destination for all things Japanese, whether you're catching an exquisitely curated exhibition in the basement gallery, browsing artisan-crafted homeware in the museum-like shop or devouring delectable sushi, skewers and sake in the smart *izakaya* (dining pub) restaurant. Hang around long enough and you'll forget you're in rainy London altogether – especially once you sample the luxurious loos, whose heated seats and bidet functions are the very definition of Japanese *omotenashi* (hospitality).

101–111 Kensington High Street, w8 5sa
Nearest station: High Street Kensington
japanhouselondon.uk

48

SWINGERS

Golf, games and grub

It might sound like a louche adult-entertainment venue, but this central London playground is every inch a family affair. Combining crazy golf, carnival games and comfort food under one roof, this 1920s resort-themed attraction promises all the fun of the seaside without the dodgy weather (or, admittedly, the sea – but then this is Oxford Circus). Grab a club and a cocktail and putt your way around the two classic nine-hole courses, before loading up your Carnival card and downing clowns, hooking ducks and whacking moles until your arms hurt. Finish with something decadent from one of the street-food beach huts, be it a 12-incher from Pizza Pilgrims, a loaded burger from Patty & Bun or a tray of super-stuffed burritos from Breddos.

15 John Prince's Street, W1G 0AB
Nearest station: Oxford Circus
swingers.club

49
ROLLER NATION

Retro indoor skating rink

When you're aching to go skating but the weather has other ideas, totter on up to Tottenham for a wheely good time. Hosting London's superlative roller discos since 2019, the capital's only purpose-built roller rink is the ultimate antidote to tempestuous weather, serving up big bops, comfort grub and free skate and equipment hire to skaters of all ages. On blustery evenings, slide on down to one of four weekly adults-only events, busting out your choice of soul, classic pop, hip-hop or house. Or grab the kids and boogie over to the ever-popular Saturday Family Jam, refuelling post-skate with hot dogs and slushies in the relaxed rink-side diner.

117 Bruce Grove, N17 6UR
Nearest station: Bruce Grove
rollernation.com

50

BABYLON PARK

Underground amusement park

Forget queuing for hours in the rain waiting to ride the Big One. This underground theme park promises all the fun of the fair whatever the weather – and even comes complete with the UK's first indoor rollercoaster. Uncannily reminiscent of *Toy Story*'s similarly space-themed Pizza Planet diner, Babylon Park caters for toddlers to teens and beyond, with its electrifying rides, compelling arcade games and out-of-this-world VR experiences, all arranged over three massive floors. For maximum fun (and the best value), prebook a timed unlimited-play slot. Then, when you're all rollercoastered out, recharge with classic fairground fare from the UFO-shaped cafe.

8 Castlehaven Road, NW1 8QU
Nearest station: Camden Town
babylonpark.com

51

BRITANNIA
LEISURE CENTRE

Wet play without the wellies

What better way to spend a rainy day with your kids than getting completely and utterly drenched? Fully shielded from the elements, this aqua-centric sports hub invites families to swap waterproofs for water wings and muddy puddles for what might just be the capital's most thrilling pool slide. Spiralling for 250+ feet, the vertiginous green flume propels kids aged 8+ (or 5+ on their adult's lap) on a dizzying white-knuckle ride, complete with selectable lighting and sound. Meanwhile, tiny thrill-seekers can splash, slide and soak themselves to their heart's content on the adjacent splash deck. Supposing you categorically can't tolerate any more moisture, take cover in the centre's cute (and delightfully dry) forest-themed soft-play space instead.

Pitfield Street, N1 5FT
Nearest station: Haggerston
better.org.uk

52

COAL DROPS YARD

Boutique shopping complex in historic buildings

We've all endured bleak, rainy-day trudges around our local shopping centre, but this upscale mall promises a far superior retail experience. Open-air, though with partially covered walkways that make shop-hopping a largely brolly-free affair, this former Victorian coal-distribution hub was the subject of a masterful redevelopment by Thomas Heatherwick in 2018 – and the result is a far cry from your average mall. Here, beneath the architectural marvel that is the dramatic 'kissing roof', you'll find everything from cult clothing brands to indie kids' stores, chi chi tattoo parlours to boutique gyms and chic bars to high-end eateries – interspersed with high-street favourites. Hungry for more? Check out the neighbouring Mare Street Market for additional shopping and sustenance in one dynamic hub.

Stable Street, N1C 4LW
Nearest station: King's Cross St Pancras
kingscross.co.uk/coal-drops-yard

53
THE HOLLY BUSH

Historic Hampstead haunt

Whether you're sitting out a rainstorm or a zombie apocalypse, this intimate Hampstead pub is the perfect place to take cover. Tucked down a cobbled street on one of north London's steepest hills, this whimsical watering hole feels delightfully clandestine – despite being a favoured celebrity spot. In the summer, customers spill onto the pavement, but it's on damp days when the pub (originally built as a house in the late 18th century) really comes into its own, with its snug assortment of lounges, complete with original panelling and open fires. Relax to the pattering of rain beneath the Tavern Bar's glass ceiling, pint of London Pride in hand, or devour something hearty from the European-inspired dining menu in the elegant Romney Room.

22 Holly Mount, NW3 6SG
Nearest station: Hampstead
hollybushhampstead.co.uk

54

BAD MOON CAFE

Tabletop gaming in railway arch

There might be a bad moon rising (or at least some black clouds forming), but it's always clear skies ahead at this friendly board game cafe. While wargaming tables occupy roughly two thirds of the space – which also hosts a well-stocked on-site shop – casual board gamers are just as warmly received by the impossibly patient staff. Book ahead to bag a spot on thundery days, then settle down with a bunch of mates, a stack of games (recommendations, tips and explanations are all readily available) and a steady flow of strategy-boosting pizza and pints. Intrigued by the intricacies of *Warhammer* or *Magic: The Gathering*? Head along to one of the regular how-to-play nights for invaluable gaming guidance.

Arch 5, 303 Holloway Road, N7 8HS
Nearest station: Holloway Road
Other location: Borough
badmooncafe.co.uk

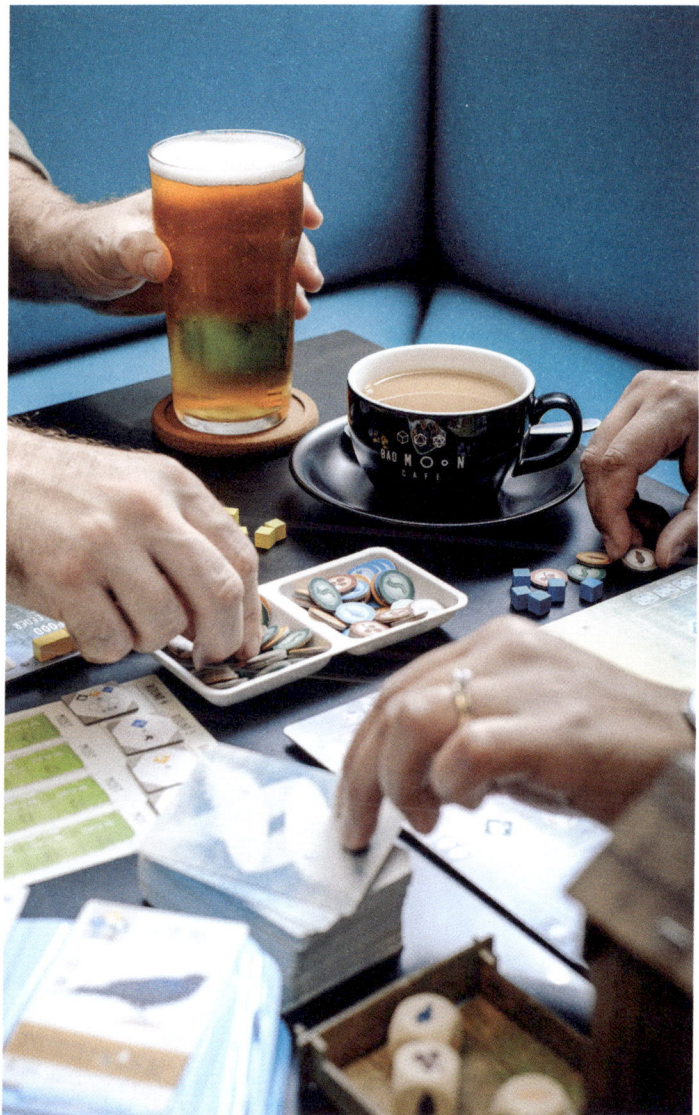

55

SOCIAL POTTERY

Friendly ceramics studio

Pottery cafes are two a penny in the capital, but few of them will brighten a miserable day like this inclusive creative studio. Established in 2015, Social Pottery boasts two exceptionally welcoming Kentish Town spaces – its hands-on pottery-making studio being conveniently located just steps from the airy painting store. At the latter, paint your choice of more than 300 pre-moulded items, spanning ceramic hamburgers to three-storey teapots; or head to the making studio for everything from wheel throwing to hand building for all ages and abilities. Feeling antisocial? Despite its name, the studio welcomes lone ceramicists just as warmly as groups, though its BYOB 'Sip and Paint' sessions are reliably one of the most enjoyable ways to pass a rainy evening with friends.

136–138 Kentish Town Road, NW1 9QB
Nearest station: Kentish Town West
Other location: White City
socialpottery.com

56

WELLCOME COLLECTION

Spotlight on health and the human experience

Its founder's name is a fitting descriptor of this tranquil museum of health, whose cluster of free-to-access public spaces offer an inspiring (and weatherproof) sanctuary to all who seek it. While built in part to house historical medical items assembled by pharmaceutical pioneer Sir Henry Wellcome, the museum feels far from dusty – its engaging, interactive exhibitions regularly platform underrepresented communities and tackle challenging topics. Once you're suitably enlightened on the idiosyncrasies of breast milk, Bedlam and body modifications (or whatever's on show this week), proceed to the library for comfy seats and further reading. Or head downstairs for light bites in the bright and buzzy cafe, via the shop for health-themed gifts.

183 Euston Road, NW1 2BE
Nearest station: Euston Square
wellcomecollection.org

57

ALFIES ANTIQUE MARKET

Vast vintage treasure trove

Bakelite brooches. Ercol nesting tables. Mary Quant boots with original labels. This eclectic emporium is an antiquarian's Shangri-La, famed far and wide for its four floors of rare and unusual vintage treasures, covering everything from fine art and furnishings to clothing and costume jewellery. Founded in 1976 in an Art Deco-style former department store, Alfies retains much of its original charm, with its labyrinthine layout and aptly vintage features, including parquet flooring and authentic interwar shop fittings. Work your way up through the warren of stalls (whose number nears 100), before admiring your spoils in the rooftop cafe over something home-cooked and hearty (don't worry, there is indoor seating – this is London, after all).

13–25 Church Street, NW8 8DT
Nearest station: Marylebone
alfiesantiques.com

Selected opinionated guides in the series:

An opinionated guide to
ACTIVE LONDON
HOXTON MINI PRESS

An opinionated guide to
ART LONDON
Spo, make time even busy spots do.
HOXTON MINI PRESS

An opinionated guide to
BIG KIDS' LONDON
The best of the capital for 5–12s
HOXTON MINI PRESS

An opinionated guide to
CALM LONDON
Places to find peace in the city
HOXTON MINI PRESS

An opinionated guide to
DESIGN LONDON
Galleries, shops, museums & more
HOXTON MINI PRESS

An opinionated guide to
EAST LONDON
4th Edition
HOXTON MINI PRESS

An opinionated guide to
ECO LONDON
Enjoy the city, love the planet
HOXTON MINI PRESS

An opinionated guide
ESCAPE LONDON
Easy trips and escapes out of the city
HOXTON MINI PRESS

An opinionated guide to
FREE LONDON
Enjoy the capital without the cash
HOXTON MINI PRESS

An opinionated guide to
HAUNTED LONDON
HOXTON MINI PRESS

An opinionated guide to
HISTORIC LONDON
HOXTON MINI PRESS

An opinionated guide to
INDEPENDENT LONDON
The Capital's Best Small Shops
HOXTON MINI PRESS

An opinionated guide to
KIDS' LONDON
The best of the capital for 0–5s
HOXTON MINI PRESS

An opinionated guide to
LITERARY LONDON
HOXTON MINI PRESS

An opinionated guide to
LONDON
HOXTON MINI PRESS

An opinionated guide to
LONDON ARCHITECTURE
HOXTON MINI PRESS

For more go to www.hoxtonminipress.com

An opinionated guide to
LONDON BOOKSHOPS

HOXTON MINI PRESS

An opinionated guide to
LONDON CHEAP EATS
Eat well, spend less

HOXTON MINI PRESS

An opinionated guide to
LONDON FOOD
The places you have to eat

HOXTON MINI PRESS

An opinionated guide to
LONDON GREEN SPACES

HOXTON MINI PRESS

An opinionated guide to
LONDON HOTELS
For the best beds, food and view

HOXTON MINI PRESS

An opinionated guide to
LONDON MARKETS

HOXTON MINI PRESS

An opinionated guide to
LONDON MUSEUMS
Nothing dusty in here

HOXTON MINI PRESS

An opinionated guide to
LONDON PUBS

HOXTON MINI PRESS

An opinionated guide to
LONDON WALKS

HOXTON MINI PRESS

An opinionated guide to
MAKE LONDON
Workshops, classes, crafts & more

HOXTON MINI PRESS

An opinionated guide to
MUSIC LONDON

HOXTON MINI PRESS

An opinionated guide to
SECRET LONDON
Wild... and safe

HOXTON MINI PRESS

An opinionated guide to
SOUTH LONDON

HOXTON MINI PRESS

An opinionated guide to
VEGAN LONDON
Third Edition

HOXTON MINI PRESS

An opinionated guide to
WEIRD LONDON
The perplexing, peculiar & delightfully odd

HOXTON MINI PRESS

An opinionated guide to
WINE LONDON
Bars, restaurants, shops & more

HOXTON MINI PRESS

IMAGE CREDITS

An Opinionated Guide to Rainy Day London
First edition, first printing

Published in 2025 by Hoxton Mini Press, London.
Copyright © Hoxton Mini Press 2025. All rights reserved.

Text by Emmy Watts
Editing by Kate Overy
Production design by Dom Grant
Production control by David Brimble
Proofreading by Florence Ward
Editorial support by Richard Enright and
    Flora MacKenzie

With thanks to Matthew Young for
initial series design.

Please note: we recommend checking the
websites listed for each entry before you
visit for the latest information on price,
opening times and pre-booking
requirements.

The right of Emmy Watts to be identified
as the creator of this Work has been
asserted under the Copyright, Designs and
Patents Act 1988.

Thank you to all of the individuals and
institutions who have provided images
and arranged permissions. While every
effort has been made to trace the present
copyright holders we apologise in advance
for any unintentional omission or error,
and would be pleased to insert the
appropriate acknowledgement in any
subsequent edition.

No part of this publication may be
reproduced, stored in a retrieval system,
or transmitted in any form or by any
means, electronic, mechanical,
photocopying, recording or otherwise,
without the prior written permission of
the copyright owner.

A CIP catalogue record for this book is
available from the British Library.

ISBN: 978-1-917719-09-4

Printed and bound by OZGraf, Poland

Manufacturer: Hoxton Mini Press, 104
Northside Studios, 16–29 Andrews Road,
London E8 4QF, UK
www.hoxtonminipress.com

Represented by: Authorised Rep
Compliance Ltd., Ground Floor, 71 Lower
Baggot Street, Dublin D02 P593, Ireland
www.arccompliance.com

Hoxton Mini Press is an environmen-
tally conscious publisher, committed
to offsetting our carbon footprint.
This book is 100 per cent carbon
compensated, with offset purchased
from Stand For Trees.

Every time you order from our website, we
plant a tree: www.hoxtonminipress.com

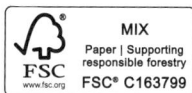

FSC
www.fsc.org

MIX
Paper | Supporting
responsible forestry
FSC® C163799

INDEX